ANIMALS AND THEIR HABITATS
Rivers, Lakes, and Wetlands

WORLD
BOOK

A Scott Fetzer company
Chicago
www.worldbookonline.com

World Book, Inc.
233 N. Michigan Avenue
Chicago, IL 60601
U.S.A.

For information about other World Book publications, visit our website at http://www.worldbookonline.com or call 1-800-WORLDBK (967-5325).

For information about sales to schools and libraries, call 1-800-975-3250 (United States), or 1-800-837-5365 (Canada).

Library of Congress Cataloging-in-Publication Data

Rivers, lakes, and wetlands.
    p. cm. -- (Animals and their habitats)
  Includes index.
  Summary: "Text and illustrations introduce several animal species that live in rivers, lakes, and wetlands. Detailed captions describe each animal, while inset maps show where the animals can be found around the world. Special features include a glossary, a climate zone map, photographs, and an index." --Provided by publisher.
  ISBN 978-0-7166-0442-6
  1. Aquatic animals--Juvenile literature. I. World Book, Inc.
  QL120.R58 2012
  591.76--dc23
                    2012005840

Animals and Their Habitats
Set ISBN: 978-0-7166-0441-9

Printed in China by Leo Paper Products LTD., Heshan, Guangdong
1st printing July 2012

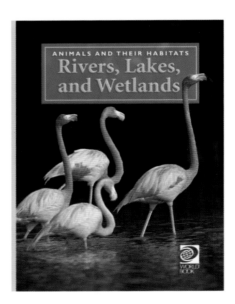

Cover image: The bright color of the greater flamingo is linked to the bird's river habitat. The feathers of adults turn pinkish-red because of a *pigment* (coloring) found in the shrimp-like animals they eat, not because of a pigment they produce themselves.

© Minden Pictures/Masterfile

Contents

Introduction

Rivers, lakes, and wetlands provide some of the richest environments on our planet. Many animals can live only in a freshwater *habitat* (the type of place where an animal lives). These habitats support abundant fish, amphibian, and insect life. Birds dive into the water from the air, while mammals plunge in from the river banks. Meanwhile, crocodiles and other *predators* (hunting animals) lurk just beneath the surface.

Freshwater habitat is found on every continent. It ranges from the merest trickle of a stream to the mightiest of rivers. The Amazon River widens to about 90 miles (140 kilometers) at its mouth, carrying more water than any other river in the world. Other freshwater habitats are wetlands, with slow-moving water and thick stands of water plants. Lakes are also vital freshwater habitats. Some are as large as inland seas.

COMMON CARP

Some freshwater animals live totally in the water. A rich variety of fish thrive in fresh waters, including catfish that can weigh more than a human being. These fish have *adaptations* (features) that enable them to find food in murky water, including fleshy barbels that act as whiskers. Many freshwater fish are flexible in their diet and other needs. This versatility has enabled such fish as the common carp to spread around much of the world, thriving in many different habitats. Mammals also live in rivers and lakes, including river dolphins. These animals use powerful sounds to find prey in the murk.

Many freshwater animals move in and out of the water. Amphibians such as frogs lay their eggs in the water, and the young develop as tadpoles. The tadpoles transform as they mature and soon come to live on land as adult frogs. A huge variety of insects lay their eggs in the water. Beetles and spiders hunt in the water. These insects and other animals draw birds that hunt from perches or dive from the surface.

HIPPOPOTAMUS

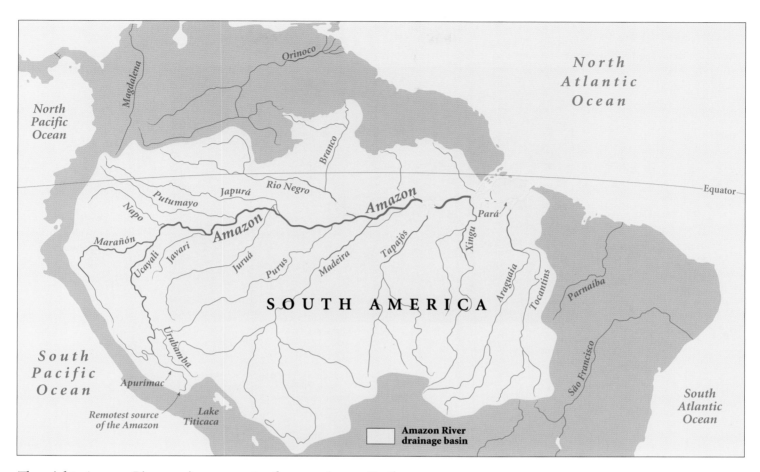

The mighty Amazon River carries more water than any river on Earth.

Other freshwater animals feed on plants. Hippopotamuses are among the largest of freshwater animals. They spend much of their time submerged in the water, with only their eyes, ears, and nostrils exposed. They feed on water plants along river banks. They share the river with mighty crocodiles, which wait in ambush to attack wildebeests. Surprisingly, hippos are a major threat to human beings, as these highly territorial mammals will flip over boats and trample intruders.

One freshwater animal creates its own habitat. The North American beaver cuts down trees to feed on wood, but it also builds dams on streams. These streams soon flood the surrounding forest, creating a freshwater pond. The pond provides safety for the beaver, which swims far better than it walks. It also provides a habitat for a tremendous variety of other animals.

AMERICAN ALLIGATOR

Wels Catfish

One of the world's largest freshwater fish, the Wels catfish can be a true monster, though it is not a danger to humans.

VITAL STATISTICS

WEIGHT	Average 100 lb (45 kg) but giants can weigh over 480 lb (220 kg)
LENGTH	About 5 ft (1.5 m), but can reach double this size
SEXUAL MATURITY	3–5 years
NUMBER OF EGGS	30,000 per kilo (2.2 lb) of body weight
HATCHING PERIOD	3–10 days, depending on water temperature
DIET	Smaller fish eat worms, crustaceans, and other fish; larger ones eat amphibians, rodents, and ducks
LIFESPAN	30 years or more

WHERE IN THE WORLD?

Ranges around the Baltic Sea, down through central, southern, and eastern Europe, extending to the Caspian Sea.

ANIMAL FACTS

These formidable *predators* (hunting animals) can simply suck their prey into their throats. They live in relatively still waters, in areas where there is a lot of submerged debris, such as tree roots, that allows them to hide away. Although their eyes are quite small, their hearing is acute which, along with their *barbels* (sensory organs), helps them to find prey easily, even in muddy waters. Warm surroundings and plentiful food supplies help to ensure their continued growth.

COLORATION
Individuals tend to be black in clear waters and brown in muddy waters.

DORSAL FIN
Located well forward on the body, the *dorsal* fin (located on the back) is small with a sharp tip.

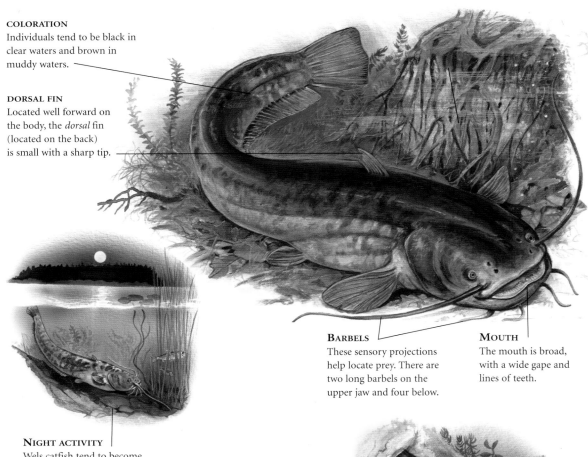

BARBELS
These sensory projections help locate prey. There are two long barbels on the upper jaw and four below.

MOUTH
The mouth is broad, with a wide gape and lines of teeth.

NIGHT ACTIVITY
Wels catfish tend to become more active after dark.

HOW BIG IS IT?

BREEDING
The male will stay with the eggs after *spawning* (laying), fanning them with his tail and guarding them until they hatch.

Common Carp

VITAL STATISTICS

WEIGHT	1–9 lb (0.5–4 kg), but can reach 44 lb (20 kg)
LENGTH	12–24 in (30–60 cm)
SEXUAL MATURITY	Females 4–5 years; males 3–5 years
NUMBER OF EGGS	About 300,000; depending on the size of the female
HATCHING INTERVAL	3 days at 25 °C (77 °F)
DIET	Bottom-feeder that sifts mud for insects, worms, snails, shrimp, fish eggs, and seeds
LIFESPAN	Up to 40–50 years

Carp are hardy fish that eat both plants and animals and can live in a variety of freshwater environments. Although carp are native to Europe, people have introduced the fish to much of the rest of the world.

WHERE IN THE WORLD?

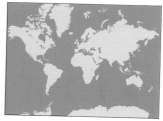

Originally found in Europe, it has now been introduced across the world.

ANIMAL FACTS

Carp feed by sucking up mud from the bottom and spitting it out into the water. Then they pick through the cloud of mud for food. This feeding behavior can be harmful to other living things. Muddy water allows less sunlight to reach *aquatic* (water) plants, limiting their growth. Many fish depend on such plants, which provide hiding places for developing young. The carp also breed in great numbers and feed on eggs. In doing so, carp can reduce the number of native fish. In North America, carp are considered a nuisance fish. But carp are a valuable food fish in Asia and Europe.

Carp eat snails and other small animals.

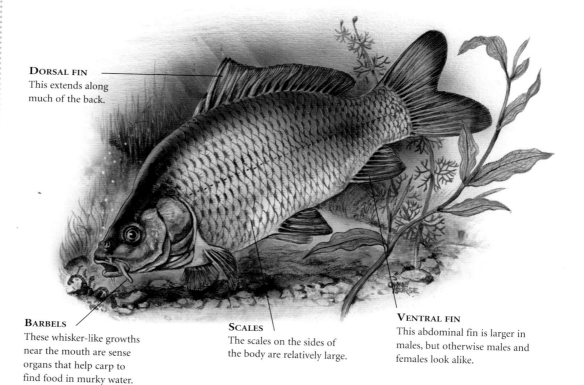

DORSAL FIN
This extends along much of the back.

BARBELS
These whisker-like growths near the mouth are sense organs that help carp to find food in murky water.

SCALES
The scales on the sides of the body are relatively large.

VENTRAL FIN
This abdominal fin is larger in males, but otherwise males and females look alike.

HOW BIG IS IT?

EGG-LAYING
The female *spawns* (lays her eggs) in shallow waters, usually in areas with abundant plants. She scatters the sticky eggs, which become attached to the plants and the muddy bottom.

Northern Pike

VITAL STATISTICS

WEIGHT	Up to 40 lb (18 kg)
LENGTH	Up to 4 ft (1.2 m)
SEXUAL MATURITY	2–3 years
NUMBER OF EGGS	35,000–300,000, depending on female size
INCUBATION PERIOD	5–26 days, depending on water temperature
DIET	Feeds on other fish, frogs, crayfish, small mammals, and birds
LIFESPAN	Up to 25 years

The northern pike is among the most fearsome of freshwater *predators* (hunting animals). It typically hides among *aquatic* (water) plants until prey comes near. Then, the fish bursts out to snatch its victim.

WHERE IN THE WORLD?

Widely distributed in the Northern Hemisphere, in Asia, Europe, and North America.

ANIMAL FACTS

The northern pike relies on stealth and speed to catch prey. The patterns on its body help it blend in with aquatic plants. Its powerful tail enables it to accelerate quickly, giving prey little chance to escape. These fish are widespread in northern regions of the world, and they are *top predators* in many areas. As a top predator, the fish feeds on a variety of animals, but nothing is able to feed on it. Only the adults are safe from predators, however, as many animals eat young pike. Also, *anglers* (people who fish) prize the adults as *game* (sport) fish, and the flesh is tasty.

Young pike grow rapidly, but only a small number become adults.

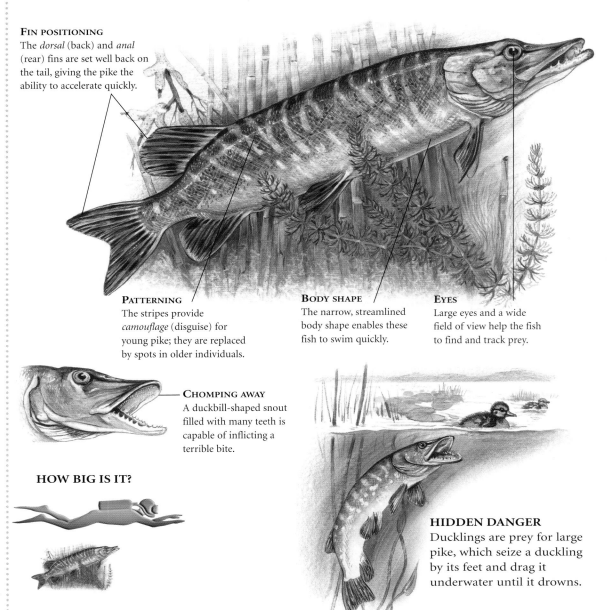

FIN POSITIONING
The *dorsal* (back) and *anal* (rear) fins are set well back on the tail, giving the pike the ability to accelerate quickly.

PATTERNING
The stripes provide *camouflage* (disguise) for young pike; they are replaced by spots in older individuals.

BODY SHAPE
The narrow, streamlined body shape enables these fish to swim quickly.

EYES
Large eyes and a wide field of view help the fish to find and track prey.

CHOMPING AWAY
A duckbill-shaped snout filled with many teeth is capable of inflicting a terrible bite.

HOW BIG IS IT?

HIDDEN DANGER
Ducklings are prey for large pike, which seize a duckling by its feet and drag it underwater until it drowns.

Three-Spined Stickleback

VITAL STATISTICS

WEIGHT	0.027 oz (0.9 g)
LENGTH	1–3 in (3–8 cm)
SEXUAL MATURITY	1–3 years
NUMBER OF EGGS	Each female lays 100–150 eggs
INCUBATION PERIOD	6–10 days
DIET	Feeds on *fish fry* (young fishes) and eggs, insects, and other tiny water animals
LIFESPAN	Up to 3 years

The three-spined stickleback has complex courtship and nesting behavior. The male builds a nest and tends the eggs. He even guards the young after they hatch.

WHERE IN THE WORLD?

Ranges widely along northern coasts, from Europe to North America in the Atlantic, and from North America to Asia in the Pacific.

ANIMAL FACTS

Few fish are as diverse as the three-spined stickleback. This fish lives in streams and rivers, lakes, marshes, and coastal waters. Their appearance varies by where they live. These fish have mating instincts as complex as those of birds. The male develops blue eyes and a red throat and belly to attract females. He builds a mound-like nest of sticks and roots and defends it from other males. After females have laid eggs in the nest, the male fans the eggs with water and protects them from *predators* (hunting animal). The male piles vegetation in the nest. After the eggs hatch, this vegetation provides a place for the hatchlings to hide and rest. The male guards the young for several more days. Such parental care is highly unusual among fish. The three-spined stickleback is plentiful. It provides food for many larger fish and birds.

SPINES
The fish gets its name from the spines found along the middle of the back. The spines make the fish hard for a predator to swallow.

IRIS
Only the breeding male has a blue iris.

UNDERPARTS
The breeding male has a red throat and belly, which attract females.

JAW STRUCTURE
Because of the animals they prey on, sticklebacks that live in shallow water have narrow jaws; fish that live in deep water have gaping jaws.

COURTSHIP DANCE

The male makes a zig-zagging display to attract a female, who responds with her own water dance. The female then enters the nest to *spawn* (lay eggs).

NESTING
The male builds a nest and defends his *territory* (personal area) from other males. Several females may lay eggs in the same nest. The male fans the eggs with water and protects them from hungry fish.

HOW BIG IS IT?

Common Mudpuppy

SPECIES • *Necturus maculosus*

VITAL STATISTICS

LENGTH	8-17 in (20-43 cm)
SEXUAL MATURITY	5–8 years
HATCHING PERIOD	Typically 38–63 days, depending on temperature; young are about 1 in (2.5 cm) at hatching
NUMBER OF EGGS	35–85 a year
DIET	Crayfish, insects, small fish, fish eggs, worms, and snails
LIFESPAN	Up to 34 years

The mudpuppy is a type of salamander that never leaves the water. It usually walks along the bottom of shallow waters on its tiny legs, though it can also swim when necessary.

WHERE IN THE WORLD?

Found in central and eastern North America.

ANIMAL FACTS

The mudpuppy is an *amphibian*, an animal that lives part of its life in the water and part on land. Most amphibians live in the water as tadpoles and then go through a *metamorphosis* (transformation of the body). They lose their *gills* (organs that absorb oxygen from the water) and develop lungs that enable them to live on land as adults. But the mudpuppy keeps its gills throughout its life. Mudpuppies are usually solitary and active at night, especially around dawn and dusk.

The gills can be fanned out to increase their surface area, helping the mudpuppy to take in more oxygen from the water.

COLORATION
The spots help break up the mudpuppy's outline in the water, enabling it to hide more easily from both *predators* (hunting animals) and prey.

GILLS
The gills are reddish because of the blood flowing through them.

LATERAL LINE
A lateral line is a row of sense organs that run down each side of the body. The organs enable the mudpuppy to sense movement in the surrounding water.

TAIL
A broad, strong tail helps the mudpuppy to swim as well as walk.

EGG-LAYING
Females lay their eggs in a nest among the rocks. They guard the nest until the eggs hatch, after about one to two months.

HOW BIG IS IT?

Common Toad

Toads are frogs, but they have broader bodies, drier skin, and shorter, less powerful back legs. Their warty skin has poisons that make them taste bad, protecting them from *predators* (hunting animals).

VITAL STATISTICS

WEIGHT	0.2–2 oz (5–55 g); *spawning* (egg-laying) females can weigh up to 4.25 oz (120 g)
LENGTH	Up to 7 in (18 cm)
SEXUAL MATURITY	4 years
HATCHING PERIOD	Tadpoles hatch after 8–10 days
NUMBER OF EGGS	600–4,000
DIET	Eats mainly insects and worms; also some small animals, such as mice
LIFESPAN:	Typically 15–20 years, but potentially up to 40 years

WHERE IN THE WORLD?

Ranges widely through western Europe, extending east as far as central Asia. Also lives in northwestern parts of Africa.

ANIMAL FACTS

Like other amphibians, toads begin life in water. In the breeding season, males gather in shallow water or at pools. They attract females with a mating call. Female toads lay their eggs in long, triple strands. Fish-like tadpoles hatch from the eggs and live in the water. As they grow, the tadpoles go through a *metamorphosis* (transformation). They lose their gills and tails. In time, they hop out of the water and live on land as adults. Toads are usually solitary. They are more active at dusk, especially on rainy evenings, seeking slugs and worms drawn from the ground by the damp weather.

The toad has a bright orange iris.

PAROTID GLANDS
These glands produce poisons that make the toad's skin taste bad.

COLORATION
Body color varies, ranging from shades of gray through sandy tones to dark brown, depending partly on the environment.

FACE
The snout is rounded, and the gaping jaws can accommodate large prey.

LEGS
During the breeding season, males develop toe swellings called *nuptial pads* that help them grasp a female or fight another male.

CATCHING PREY
The common toad has a long, sticky tongue. The tongue shoots out to snatch an insect, then pulls it back into the mouth—all in an instant!

HOW BIG IS IT?

Natterjack Toad

VITAL STATISTICS

WEIGHT	Averages about 0.7 oz (20 g)
LENGTH	2–2.5 in (6–7 cm)
SEXUAL MATURITY	2–3 years
HATCHING PERIOD	7–12 days; hatching takes longer in cold weather
NUMBER OF EGGS	Up to 2,600
DIET	Hunts mainly insects, worms, slugs, and other small animals
LIFESPAN	Up to 12 years

The male natterjack toad has a loud mating call. He is able to inflate a *vocal sac* (folds of skin) under the chin, which makes his calls much louder. The calls attract females to warm, shallow pools to breed.

WHERE IN THE WORLD?

Lives in western and northern Europe, from Portugal to Ireland and as far north as Estonia and southern Sweden.

ANIMAL FACTS

Natterjack toads are usually solitary, and they are spread thinly through the countryside. The loud calls of the males carry over a wide distance, helping the toads gather to breed. The breeding season comes in the late spring and early summer. The toads gather at warm, shallow pools, where the females lay strands of eggs. The pools may evaporate over the summer, killing the tadpoles before they can become adults. However, the toads may breed several times a season in different locations. This behavior ensures that some tadpoles will survive to become adults.

The male inflates a sac on its throat to make its loud mating call even louder.

STRIPING
A distinctive yellow stripe runs down the middle of the back, making these toads easy to identify.

LEGS
Natterjacks have longer legs than many other toads, so they tend to walk rather than hop, leaving distinctive tracks in sand.

EYES
The iris is a yellowish color surrounding a black pupil.

BODY
Wart-like swellings cover the body.

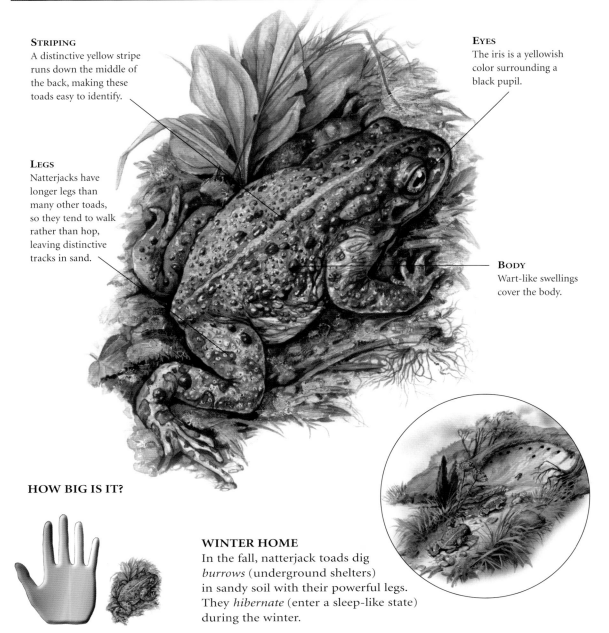

HOW BIG IS IT?

WINTER HOME
In the fall, natterjack toads dig *burrows* (underground shelters) in sandy soil with their powerful legs. They *hibernate* (enter a sleep-like state) during the winter.

Common Midwife Toad

SPECIES • *Alytes obstetricans*

Midwife toads are unusual among *amphibians* (cold-blooded animals) in that their eggs develop outside of water. The male carries the eggs around on his back until they are ready to hatch.

VITAL STATISTICS

LENGTH	About 2 in (5 cm) long; females are generally larger than males
SEXUAL MATURITY	2 years
HATCHING PERIOD	3–6 weeks; they may remain as tadpoles over the winter
NUMBER OF EGGS	Up to about 50 per *spawning* (egg laying)
DIET	Eats mainly insects, slugs, and worms
LIFESPAN	7–10 years

WHERE IN THE WORLD?

Found in Portugal and Spain, through France to Belgium, the Netherlands, Germany, and Switzerland. It has been introduced to the United Kingdom.

ANIMAL FACTS

The egg-carrying behavior of the male midwife toad helps to protect the eggs from being eaten. This toad produces fewer eggs than many other amphibians, because more of the eggs it produces will survive. The male keeps the eggs moist until they are ready to hatch. Then, it takes the eggs to a shallow pool, where the tadpoles will swim and grow. After several months, the tadpoles go through a *metamorphosis* (transformation) and become adults that live on land. If threatened, the toad fills itself with air, trying to make itself appear larger. Like other toads, the midwife toad also has *glands* (organs) that make poisons. These poisons make the toad taste bad. In fact, *predators* (hunting animals) that eat the toad may become sick or even die.

EGG MASS
Males can carry up to 150 eggs at once, from as many as three different females.

TYMPANUM
This round area serves as an eardrum, transmitting sounds to the inner ear.

APPEARANCE
Gray overall, with red, wart-like swellings usually visible on the sides of the body.

EYES
The eyes are large, with a vertical, slit-shaped pupil.

HOW BIG IS IT?

HAZARDOUS WATER

Tadpoles face a variety of predators in the water, including dragonfly *larvae* (young). However, the tadpoles can eventually reach up to 3.5 inches (9 centimeters) long. At that point, dragonfly larvae no longer pose a serious threat.

European Tree Frog

SPECIES • *Hyla arborea*

VITAL STATISTICS

LENGTH	1.25–2 in (3–5 cm)
SEXUAL MATURITY	1 year
HATCHING PERIOD	About 3 weeks
NUMBER OF EGGS	200–2,000 in total, laid in smaller batches
DIET	Hunts a variety of small animals, including flies and butterflies
LIFESPAN	3–5 years on average

Tree frogs are great climbers that use their powerful hind legs to make long leaps. This leaping ability helps the European tree frog catch flies and other fast-flying insects.

WHERE IN THE WORLD?

Found in much of Europe, northern Africa, and east into Asia.

ANIMAL FACTS

Despite its name, the European tree frog can also live on bushes and other vegetation. In wetlands, it climbs reeds and other shrubs. If threatened, the tree frog can leap into the water to make a quick escape. Males call at the start of the breeding season, forming a chorus as they compete against each other in song. Their calls are said to resemble the quacking of a duck. In the winter, the tree frog *hibernates* (enters a sleep-like state), often under rocks or leaf piles. Unfortunately, the number of these frogs is falling. They face a variety of threats, including destruction of forests and wetlands. The frogs are also harmed by pollution of the waters in which they lay their eggs and grow as tadpoles.

COLORATION
The color varies between gray, green, and tan, depending on the temperature and the frog's mood. Males have brownish-yellow *vocal sacs* (folds of skin) that amplify the frog's call.

PATTERN
The dark stripe running through the eyes can vary in color from pale brown to black.

CAMOUFLAGE
The frog may hunch down low to blend in more effectively against a leaf.

TOES
Expanded discs on the tips of the toes are sticky, helping these frogs to climb easily.

The underside of the body is whitish.

HOW BIG IS IT?

STAYING ALIVE

Their powerful hind legs enable these frogs to jump well, helping them to escape from herons and other *predators* (hunting animals).

Common Spadefoot Toad

VITAL STATISTICS

LENGTH	2–4 in (5–10 cm)
SEXUAL MATURITY	Less than a year
HATCHING PERIOD	Lasts 2–3 days
NUMBER OF EGGS	10–500, with *spawning* (egg laying) occurring after heavy rainfall
DIET	Insects, worms, spiders, and other small animals
LIFESPAN	Up to 13 years

This toad has sharp-edged, spade-like growths on its hind feet that enable it to dig quickly, especially in the loose, sandy soils it favors. When threatened, the toad digs a *burrow* (underground shelter) to escape.

WHERE IN THE WORLD?

Lives in central Europe, from eastern France up to southern parts of Sweden, and east through western Asia as far as Iran.

ANIMAL FACTS

The common spadefoot toad can escape danger in ways other than digging into the soil. It can also release an unpleasant liquid that smells a bit like garlic. For this reason, the toad is also known as "the garlic frog." The smelly liquid may disgust some *predators* (hunting animals), giving the toad time to escape. The toad can also give a harsh shriek, which may startle a predator into dropping the toad. The toad breeds in shallow pools that form after heavy rainfall. These pools soon dry out, so the tadpoles develop quickly, reaching adult form in as little as two weeks. Despite its name, this animal is actually a frog.

COLORATION
Variable yellowish and brownish patterning helps these toads to blend in with vegetation.

FEET
Only the hind feet have the large spade that enables this toad to dig quickly.

SKIN
The skin is moist rather than dry and warty like that of true toads.

FACE
Large, rounded jaws are used to seize earthworms and other prey.

The spade on the hind leg enables the toad to dig well.

HOW BIG IS IT?

KEEPING WATCH
The spadefoot toad burrows with its hind feet, so it can watch for danger as it digs.

American Bullfrog

VITAL STATISTICS

WEIGHT	Up to 1 lb (0.5 kg)
LENGTH	As much as 8 in (20 cm); females are larger than males
SEXUAL MATURITY	3–5 years
HATCHING PERIOD	3–5 days on average, longer in cold weather
NUMBER OF EGGS	Up to 40,000 at a single *spawning* (egg laying)
DIET	Eats insects, spiders, worms, and such small animals as frogs and snakes
LIFESPAN	8–10 years in the wild

ANIMAL FACTS

The American bullfrog lives in or near ponds and gentle streams, usually along the shoreline. This location provides the frog with a way to escape from danger, by leaping into the water. Adult males strongly defend their *territory* (personal area) and will wrestle one another for control of a bit of shore. The male's loud call carries over the countryside, attracting females. The female lays thousands of tiny eggs, which hatch after only a few days. However, it can take up to three years for the tadpoles to change into adult frogs. The tadpoles have a bad taste, and most fish will not eat them. But a variety of animals feed on the adults, including herons, snakes, and raccoons. People also eat the delicate white flesh of the hind legs.

The American bullfrog is the largest frog in North America. Its name comes from the male's mating call, which sounds like the roar of a bull. The males sound as though they are saying "jug-o-rum."

WHERE IN THE WORLD?

Native to eastern North America, as far west as the Rockies. It has been introduced to California, South America, and areas of Asia and Europe.

COLORATION
Coloring varies by region and temperature, with cold temperatures causing a darker coloration.

HIND LEGS
Hind legs are usually banded, as in this case.

TYMPANUM
This patch of skin serves as an eardrum and is larger on the male, providing a way to distinguish the sexes.

MOUTH
A wide gape allows the bullfrog to take large prey.

WATERY ESCAPE
Bullfrogs stay close to water. They use their powerful hind legs to leap into the water at any hint of danger.

HOW BIG IS IT?

Gavial

SPECIES • *Gavialis gangeticus*

VITAL STATISTICS

WEIGHT	350–400 lb (159–181 kg); males are heavier
LENGTH	20 ft (6 m)
SEXUAL MATURITY	About 10 years, at 9.8 ft (3 m) long
NUMBER OF EGGS	30–50 per clutch
INCUBATION PERIOD	Around 90 days
DIET	Adults feed on fish; the young eat insects, frogs, and other small animals
LIFESPAN	40–60 years

The gavial belongs to a large group of reptiles called crocodilians. The gavial hunts for fish with its long snout. It often hunts in the bends of rivers, where the water is deep and the current is slower.

WHERE IN THE WORLD?

Found in India and Nepal, but now extinct in Bhutan, Bangladesh, Myanmar (also called Burma), and Pakistan.

ANIMAL FACTS

The gavial is among the largest of the *crocodilians* (a type of reptile). It is graceful and fast in the water, which it rarely leaves. It may climb out onto riverbanks or sand-bars to bask in the sun. As a reptile, the gavial is *cold-blooded,* meaning its body temperature varies with the environment. The gavial is highly *endangered* (at risk of dying out). Fewer than 300 adults are thought to survive in the wild. They face many threats. These include *poaching* (illegal hunting), water pollution, and the theft of their eggs. The animals are also at risk from dams, which may flood their *habitat* (living place). Fishing nets kill many gavials, and fishing reduces the food available to them.

SNOUT
The swelling on the tip of a male's snout is called a *ghara*, because it resembles an Indian pot with that shape.

JAWS
More than 100 sharp teeth prevent fish from escaping from the gavial's mouth.

NESTING
The female digs a nest in a sandy riverbank. She guards the nest and later the young that hatch.

COLORATION
Adults are a darker shade of olive than the young.

TAIL
Long and flattened, the tail propels the gavial through the water.

The male (top) has a swelling on his snout, which the female (bottom) lacks.

HOW BIG IS IT?

FISHING STRATEGY
Gavials catch fish by moving their long snouts from side to side. When they snag a fish, they turn it head-first and gulp it down.

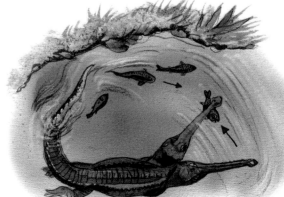

Nile Crocodile

This fearsome reptile hunts on land but prefers to ambush its prey in the water. It lurks just beneath the surface, then lunges forward to seize the prey in its powerful jaws, dragging its victim to a watery death.

VITAL STATISTICS

WEIGHT	About 500 lb (225 kg); males are heavier
LENGTH	11–18 ft (3.3–5.5 m)
SEXUAL MATURITY	About 10 years, at 9.8 ft (3 m) long
NUMBER OF EGGS	25–80 per clutch
INCUBATION PERIOD	Around 90 days
DIET	Adults feed on birds, fish, mammals, and reptiles, including animals as large as wildebeests
LIFESPAN	70–90 years

WHERE IN THE WORLD?

Found throughout most of Africa south of the Sahara, extending into Egypt in the east, reaching parts of western Madagascar.

ANIMAL FACTS

Nile crocodiles are *top predators* (hunting animals) in Africa, taking a variety of prey. They can hunt on land, but they usually ambush prey from the water. Their flattened body enables them to lurk with just their eyes above the surface. Animals such as wildebeets, which must cross rivers to find fresh grass, are among the crocodile's many victims. In fact, these crocodiles are among the few animals that eat people. Nile crocodiles may kill hundreds or even thousands of people in rural areas of Africa. The Nile crocodile was nearly wiped out by human hunting, until legal protection allowed its numbers to recover. It remains *threatened* (in danger of being wiped out) in many areas of Africa.

AMBUSH HUNTER
Crocodiles can burst from the water without warning to seize prey. They can twist a large animal into pieces by rapidly spinning lengthwise in the water.

SCUTES
The back is armored with bony scales known as scutes (pronounced *skyootz*).

FEET
The toes are equipped with strong claws.

JAWS
These are incredibly powerful, biting with a force of 3,000 pounds per square inch (210 kilograms per square centimeter), enough to bite through many types of concrete.

HOW BIG IS IT?

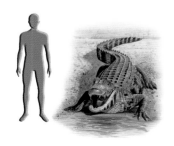

TENDER PARENTS

A young crocodile emerges from its leathery egg, which is a bit larger than a chicken egg. The parents guard their nests and may roll the eggs in their mouths to help the babies hatch. The mother collects the hatchlings in her mouth and carries them to water. She guards her young for a year or more.

American Alligator

VITAL STATISTICS

WEIGHT	450–550 lb (200–249 kg); males are much bigger
LENGTH	Usually 10–15 ft (3–4 m)
SEXUAL MATURITY	About 10 years, at 9.8 ft (3 m) long
NUMBER OF EGGS	25–60 per clutch
INCUBATION PERIOD	Around 63 days
DIET	Adults eat mainly fish, small mammals, snakes, and turtles
LIFESPAN	40–60 years

ANIMAL FACTS

Alligators are the most vocal of the crocodilians. They roar and bellow and slap their jaws on the water. Female alligators lay their eggs in the spring and cover them with a mound of rotting leaves, which gives off heat. The newly hatched young call to their mother with high-pitched yelps. The mother scratches open the nest and frees them. Although the mother tries to protect her young, most are eaten by birds, raccoons, and other *predators* (hunting animals). Alligators were nearly wiped out by hunting in the 1900's. Legal protection has allowed their numbers to recover. Alligators are also raised on farms for their meat and hides.

Alligators thrive in swamps and other wetlands.

In winter, American alligators rest underwater in deep holes called 'gator holes that they make with their bodies. During droughts, 'gator holes may be an important refuge for fish, frogs, and other animals.

WHERE IN THE WORLD?

Lives in the southeastern United States, especially Florida and Louisiana.

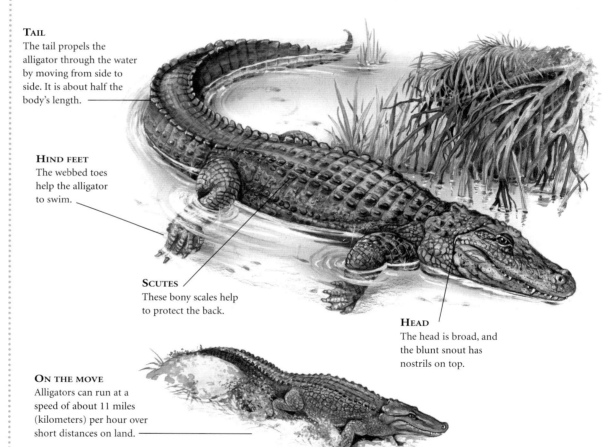

TAIL
The tail propels the alligator through the water by moving from side to side. It is about half the body's length.

HIND FEET
The webbed toes help the alligator to swim.

SCUTES
These bony scales help to protect the back.

HEAD
The head is broad, and the blunt snout has nostrils on top.

ON THE MOVE
Alligators can run at a speed of about 11 miles (kilometers) per hour over short distances on land.

HOW BIG IS IT?

ALLIGATOR OR CROCODILE?

The lower fourth tooth of a crocodile grows extra long and fits into a groove in the side of the upper jaw (right, top). The tooth remains visible when the jaws are closed. In an alligator, this tooth fits into a pocket of the upper jaw and disappears when the jaw is closed (right, bottom).

Green Anaconda

VITAL STATISTICS

WEIGHT	Up to about 450 lb (205 kg); females are much larger
LENGTH	Average 20 ft (6 m), but some reach up to 30 ft (9 m) long
SEXUAL MATURITY	Females 3 years; males 18 months
INCUBATION PERIOD	6–7 months
NUMBER OF OFFSPRING	20–100
DIET	Eats mainly fish, snakes, crocodilians, and capybara; large snakes may take deer and peccaries
LIFESPAN	10–30 years

ANIMAL FACTS

The green anaconda is active at night and spends most of its time in the water. Apart from prey they catch in the water, these snakes also seize animals that come to drink, attacking from the water without warning. Their hunting at night is aided by heat-sensing pits along their lips. These pits enable them to detect the body heat of *mammals* (animals that feed their young on the mother's milk). After eating a large meal, the snake may go weeks or even months without eating. Attacks on human beings are rare.

Anacondas have 100 backward-pointing teeth that help them to grasp prey.

The green anaconda is one of the largest of all snakes. Like other giant snakes, it is a constrictor—it suffocates its prey by squeezing it in its muscular coils.

WHERE IN THE WORLD?

Found in South America east of the Andes, spread throughout the Amazon and Orinoco river basins.

COLORATION
The anaconda's coloration helps it to blend in with river water. The underparts are yellowish.

SKULL
The bones in the skull are highly flexible. This enables the snake to swallow large prey.

SPURS
Present near the tail, these are the tiny remains of what were once hind legs.

PATTERNING
The black blotches on these snakes are variable, allowing individuals to be identified.

HOW BIG IS IT?

LIVE BIRTH

A female anaconda carries her eggs inside her body. The young hatch just before they are born. Incredibly, females can give birth to up to 100 young. The mother may lose half her body weight after giving birth.

Red-Eared Slider

This turtle is called a "slider" because it often basks on riverbanks but slip backs into the water if danger threatens. It is the most popular kind of pet turtle in the United States.

VITAL STATISTICS

WEIGHT	1.5–3.0 lb (0.6–1.5 g)
LENGTH	5–11 in (13–28 cm)
SEXUAL MATURITY	Females 5–7 years; males 3–5 years
NUMBER OF EGGS	4–23; 1–3 clutches laid over the summer
INCUBATION PERIOD	60–75 days; breeds from March to July
DIET	Feeds on *aquatic* (water) plants, crayfish, fish, insects, and other small animals
LIFESPAN	Up to 30 years

WHERE IN THE WORLD?

Found in North America in the Mississippi River Valley, from Illinois to the Gulf of Mexico and west into Kansas and Oklahoma.

ANIMAL FACTS

Like other reptiles, the red-eared slider is *cold-blooded,* meaning that its body temperature varies with the environment. As a result, it often basks in the sun to warm up. In fact, several turtles may crowd onto a log to bask together. Adults are safe from most *predators* (hunting animals) because they can withdraw into their tough shell. However, slider eggs and hatchlings are eaten by many animals, including raccoons, skunks, opossums, and foxes. The popularity of these turtles as pets has caused their spread to other parts of the world, where they may threaten native wildlife.

HIDING AWAY
The turtles often hang near the surface of the water, hiding under plant cover.

SHELL
As the turtle grows, the *scutes* (hard, bony shells) covering the different sections of the shell peel off.

HIND FEET
These provide the main propulsive thrust when the turtle is swimming.

RED STRIPE
These turtles usually have a characteristic red stripe behind the eye.

FRONT FEET
Mature males have much longer front claws than females do. The claws may be used in battles with other males to gain or defend their *territory* (personal area).

COURTSHIP
The male also uses its long claws to fan water over the face of the female in a kind of watery caress.

The shell of a hatchling (left) darkens as the turtle grows to adulthood (right).

HOW BIG IS IT?

Common Snapping Turtle

The common snapping turtle is one of the largest freshwater turtles. Its long, flexible neck and powerful, beak-like jaws make it a fearsome *predator* (hunting animal), though it also eats plants.

VITAL STATISTICS

WEIGHT	9–35 lb (4–16 kg)
LENGTH	8–18 in (20–45 cm) across the center of the shell; tail is almost as long as body
SEXUAL MATURITY	7–9 years
NUMBER OF EGGS	20–80, round and white
INCUBATION PERIOD	9–18 weeks
DIET	Eats aquatic plants, ducks, fish, frogs, insects, rodents, mussels, salamanders snails, turtles, and worms
LIFESPAN	30–50 years

WHERE IN THE WORLD?

Found in North America, from southern Alberta across to Nova Scotia and south across the United States to the Gulf of Mexico and west to central Texas.

ANIMAL FACTS

The snapping turtle is known for its fierce attitude. It will not hesitate to snap at an animal that disturbs it. This ferocity may result from the fact that its head and legs are too large to pull back into the shell. Thus, it cannot simply wait out an attack from the safety of its shell. However, the turtle still tries to escape into the water whenever possible. Some people keep snapping turtles as pets, but they are difficult to handle and can deliver painful bites. Some people eat the flesh of this turtle, using it to make turtle soup.

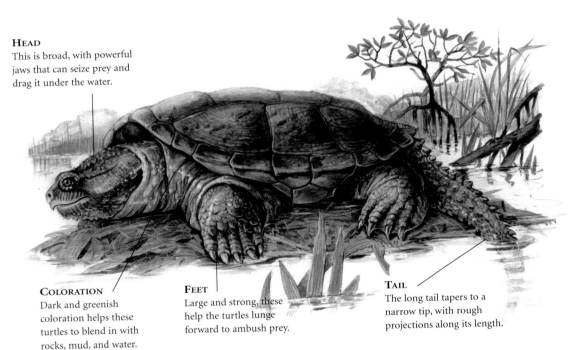

HEAD
This is broad, with powerful jaws that can seize prey and drag it under the water.

COLORATION
Dark and greenish coloration helps these turtles to blend in with rocks, mud, and water.

FEET
Large and strong, these help the turtles lunge forward to ambush prey.

TAIL
The long tail tapers to a narrow tip, with rough projections along its length.

MOUTHPARTS
Although turtles do not have teeth, their hooked, beak-like jaws can slice through flesh easily.

DEVELOPMENT
The leathery egg protects the growing turtle within, allowing oxygen to enter the egg but preventing loss of moisture.

The claws on the feet are useful for digging.

HOW BIG IS IT?

Great Diving Beetle

SPECIES • *Dyticus marginalis*

LENGTH	1.4 in (3.5 cm)
NUMBER OF EGGS	20, deposited in the stems of *aquatic* (water) plants
DEVELOPMENT PERIOD	Hatching in 2–3 weeks; *larval* (early) stage lasts 6–8 weeks; may overwinter as *pupae* (inactive stage)
HABITAT	Ponds and slow-flowing water, also seen on land
DIET	Eats insects, tadpoles, and small fish
LIFESPAN	2–3 years

This aggressive beetle does not hesitate to attack *aquatic* (water) creatures larger than itself. It will even take on small fish and tadpoles. It favors waters with dense plant growth.

WHERE IN THE WORLD?

Found throughout much of Europe extending across northern Asia.

ANIMAL FACTS

This beetle spends most of its time in the water, hunting for prey. Before it dives, it traps air bubbles under its *elytra* (front wing covers). These air bubbles allow the beetle to breathe oxygen while it is under water. Despite its size, the beetle is also able to fly, by lifting its elytra and moving its rear wings. The beetle flies only at night, when it can use reflections of moonlight to spot fresh water. Today, the beetles are often drawn to street lights by mistake. It is best not to handle the great diving beetle. Although it is not dangerous to people, the beetle's mouthparts can give a painful nip.

The wing covers are raised during flight.

LEGS
There are three pairs of legs; the longest and most powerful are the hind pair.

COLORATION
Most of the body is brownish-black, with light borders.

MOUTHPARTS
These are powerful, enabling the beetle to rip apart its prey.

ELYTRA
These hard coverings on the front wings help protect the beetle's body and delicate rear wings. Ridges on the elytra indicate a female. The covers are smooth in males.

ANTENNAE
The long antennae sense both movements and odors in the water.

HOW BIG IS IT?

GETTING AROUND
These beetles rely on their hind legs when swimming, moving them together like oars.

Emperor Dragonfly

SPECIES • *Anax imperator*

The emperor dragonfly is one of the largest "hawker" dragonflies. These dragonflies hunt by swooping down on insect prey in flight, the way a hawk hunts smaller birds.

VITAL STATISTICS

LENGTH	About 3 in (7.8 cm); wingspan up to 4 in (10.5 cm)
EGGS	Up to 500
DEVELOPMENTAL PERIOD	Cream-colored eggs hatch after 3 weeks; *nymphs* (young) spend 2 years in the water before becoming adults
DIET	Nymphs hunt *fish fry* (young fish) and tadpoles; adults catch flies and butterflies
LIFESPAN	Adult dragonflies live about 4 weeks

WHERE IN THE WORLD?

Lives throughout much of Europe, into the Middle East and northwestern India. Also present in parts of Africa.

ANIMAL FACTS

Dragonflies are among the fastest flying insects. Their four large wings make them graceful fliers and enable them to catch other insects in mid-air. The dragonfly has six legs covered with spines. As a dragonfly flies, it holds its legs together to form a basket for capturing insects. The dragonfly grabs hold of its prey with its legs or jaws. It may eat the prey while flying. Adult dragonflies do not live for long. Their main purpose is to mate and lay eggs. Females lay their eggs in weedy areas of water. The *nymphs* (young without fully developed wings) that hatch spend two years feeding in the water. They *molt* (shed their skin) several times as they grow. Finally, they climb out of the water and molt a last time. The adult dragonfly soon flies away.

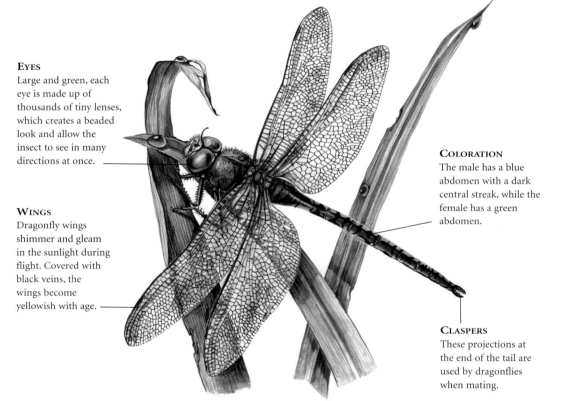

EYES
Large and green, each eye is made up of thousands of tiny lenses, which creates a beaded look and allow the insect to see in many directions at once.

WINGS
Dragonfly wings shimmer and gleam in the sunlight during flight. Covered with black veins, the wings become yellowish with age.

COLORATION
The male has a blue abdomen with a dark central streak, while the female has a green abdomen.

CLASPERS
These projections at the end of the tail are used by dragonflies when mating.

NYMPHS
The nymphs feed on a variety of small animals, including tadpoles and fish fry. The nymphs spend about two years in the water before they mature into flying adults.

HOW BIG IS IT?

Broad-Bodied Chaser

SPECIES • *Libellula depressa*

The broad-bodied chaser is among the most common dragonflies of Europe and western Asia. It is a common sight in gardens. "Chaser" dragonflies lurk on plants and then dash out to catch prey.

VITAL STATISTICS

LENGTH	3 in (7.8 cm); wingspan 2.8 in (7 cm)
EGGS	Laid singly
DEVELOPMENTAL PERIOD	Eggs hatch after 2–3 weeks; the brown *nymph* (young) spends 1–3 years in the water
DIET	Nymphs hunt small water animals; adults hunt winged insects
LIFESPAN	Up to 4 weeks

WHERE IN THE WORLD?

Found across much of Europe, east into central Asia and the Middle East.

ANIMAL FACTS

The male broad-bodied chaser will chase and attack any other male that enters its *territory* (personal area). It attempts to mate with females that come near. Mating occurs in mid-flight. After mating, the female deposits her eggs among nearby *aquatic* (water) plants. Meanwhile, the male hovers nearby, ready to alert its mate to such dangers as hungry birds. The aquatic vegetation provides cover for the *nymphs* (young without fully developed wings), which take one to three years to grow into adults. Chasers are stocky dragonflies that can be identified by the dark areas at the base of the wings. The stocky appearance and flight patterns of chasers resemble those of wasps. But dragonflies do not have stingers.

APPEARANCE
The stocky and relatively short body shape of these dragonflies aids identification.

COLORATION
The male has a blue abdomen edged with yellow. Females have a brown abdomen with yellow stripes.

LEGS
Segmented and relatively thin, the legs allow the dragonfly to cling to vegetation.

WING MARKINGS
Short, black bars mark the leading edge of the wings, near the wing tips.

HOW BIG IS IT?

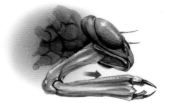

A DEADLY CATCH
These dragonflies are equipped with strong claws that spring out during flight, enabling them to seize prey from the air.

European Water Spider

VITAL STATISTICS

LENGTH	0.4–0.6 in (0.9–1.5 cm); males are larger than females, which is unusual in spiders
SEXUAL MATURITY	Likely to be around 6 months
HATCHING PERIOD	Probably averages about 3 weeks
NUMBER OF EGGS	30–70, laid in the upper part of the female's bell
DIET	Insects, mites, and shrimp
LIFESPAN	Up to about 2 years

The water spider is the only spider known to live entirely underwater. It carries air bubbles from the surface to fill an underwater web, which acts as a "diving bell," from which the spider hunts.

WHERE IN THE WORLD?

Found throughout Europe and northern Asia, as far east as Japan. They also occur in Africa, north of the Sahara.

ANIMAL FACTS

Like a diving bell, the spider's underwater web relies on air pressure to keep water out. Yet, the underwater web does more than hold air. Extending into the water, it also picks up vibrations made by prey, much like a spider web in the air. The female relies on her web more than the male, who is an active hunter. The spiders must sometimes come to the surface to collect fresh air for the web. However, the web also acts as a *gill* (oxygen-absorbing organ), allowing oxygen to pass from the water into the bell. These spiders must live in relatively calm waters, so that the bell is not swept away by currents.

The water spider has large mouthparts and several eyes.

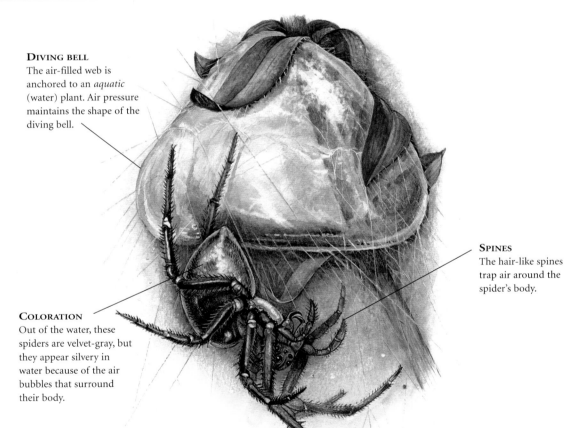

DIVING BELL
The air-filled web is anchored to an *aquatic* (water) plant. Air pressure maintains the shape of the diving bell.

SPINES
The hair-like spines trap air around the spider's body.

COLORATION
Out of the water, these spiders are velvet-gray, but they appear silvery in water because of the air bubbles that surround their body.

HOW BIG IS IT?

UNDERWATER BREEDING
The male builds a diving bell next to the female's home. Then, he builds a tunnel to reach her. After mating, she lays her eggs inside her diving bell.

Amazon River Dolphin

SPECIES • *Inia geoffrensis*

The Amazon river dolphin is also known as the "pink dolphin," for the way its skin takes on a reddish hue as it matures. Locally, it is known as the *boto,* which is short for *red dolphin* in Portuguese.

VITAL STATISTICS

WEIGHT	200–400 lb (90–181 kg); males are slightly bigger
LENGTH	6–9 ft (1.8–2.7 m);
SEXUAL MATURITY	5–7 years
LENGTH OF PREGNANCY	Up to 365 days
NUMBER OF OFFSPRING	1; *weaning* (to stop nursing on mother's milk) probably occurs within a year
DIET	Eats mainly fish, including catfish and piranhas; also feeds on crabs and turtles
LIFESPAN	Up to 30 years

WHERE IN THE WORLD?

Found throughout the Amazon river basin, in northern and central South America. Also present in the Orinoco River.

ANIMAL FACTS

The Amazon river dolphin is usually solitary. The largest river dolphin, it feeds almost entirely on fish. Like other dolphins, it locates prey using reflected sounds, an ability called *echolocation.* This ability is especially useful in muddy river water. The dolphin's beak also has sensitive hairs that act like whiskers. Scientists believe that the number of these dolphins is falling. Dams and loss of forests have damaged rivers. Fishermen have also killed many dolphins, often catching them by accident.

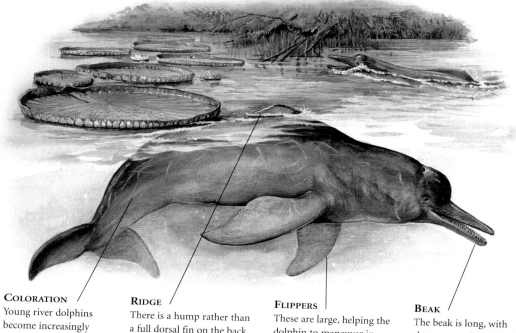

COLORATION
Young river dolphins become increasingly pinkish as they mature.

RIDGE
There is a hump rather than a full dorsal fin on the back, which may be seen breaking the water surface.

FLIPPERS
These are large, helping the dolphin to maneuver in shallow water with many *aquatic* (water) plants.

BEAK
The beak is long, with sharp, cone-shaped teeth.

Crocodilians sometimes prey on river dolphins.

HOW BIG IS IT?

WATER WORLD

Some areas of the forest flood in the wet season, enabling dolphins to venture out onto the flood plains. Females with young linger on the flood plains, where slow currents and few *predators* (hunting animals) give the young a chance to grow.

Manatee

The manatee is a large mammal that is usually found in shallow coastal waters, though it also ventures into rivers. It feeds entirely on sea grass and other *aquatic* (water) vegetation.

VITAL STATISTICS

WEIGHT	Up to 3,500 lb (1,600 kg); females are usually larger
LENGTH	Up to 13 ft (4 m)
SEXUAL MATURITY	8–18 years
LENGTH OF PREGNANCY	About 12 months
NUMBER OF OFFSPRING	1; young suckle upside down beneath their mother's body; weaning occurs at 12–18 months
DIET	Grazes on a variety of sea grasses and aquatic vegetation
LIFESPAN	Up to 60 years

ANIMAL FACTS

Like other *mammals* (animals whose young feed on the mother's milk), manatees must come to the surface to breathe. Manatees also have many unusual characteristics. Their bones are solid and heavy, and their lungs extend through much of the body. These features help them to maintain their position in the water. Manatees are also sensitive to cold. They cannot survive in water that is colder than 68 °F (20 °C). Manatees usually swim slowly, at about 5 miles (8 kilometers) per hour. Manatees are too slow to move out of the way of a speeding motorboat, and boaters may not see the gentle mammals until it is too late. Many manatees have been killed by speedboats. Others have scars from propellers. Laws restrict the speed of boats in some areas where manatees live.

WHERE IN THE WORLD?

Ranges from the southeastern coasts of North America, through the Caribbean, along the east coast of Central America, as far south as northern Brazil.

TEETH
Teeth are replaced from behind as they wear down. Manatees typically only have six grinding teeth.

FLIPPERS
The flippers have nails on the end, showing that the animal's ancestors lived on land.

WATER GRAZERS
Manatees favor the shallow water where aquatic plants grow, often at depths of 7 feet (2 meters) or less.

A PRIMITIVE TRUNK
The upper lip is divided into two parts, helping the manatee to grasp water plants.

TAIL
The rounded, paddle-shaped tail pushes the manatee through the water. The animal cannot swim quickly.

HOW BIG IS IT?

FEEDING HABITS

Manatees uproot sea grass, holding it with their flippers as they graze. They tend to visit the same sea grass beds regularly, for sea grass that grows back after grazing has more protein and nutrients.

Hippopotamus

VITAL STATISTICS

WEIGHT	2,500–3,000 lb (1,130–1,400 kg); can weigh up to 5,800 lb (2,630 kg)
LENGTH	12–15 ft (4–5 m), up to about 5 ft (1.5 m) tall
SEXUAL MATURITY	Females 4–10 years; males 7–12 years
LENGTH OF PREGNANCY	About 248 days; weaning occurs 6–8 months later
NUMBER OF OFFSPRING	1
DIET	Grazes on grass and water plants
LIFESPAN	Typically 30–40 years

The hippopotamus is well suited to life in the water. Its ears, eyes, and nostrils remain exposed even when the rest of the head is underwater. The hippo can also close its nostrils and ears when it dives.

WHERE IN THE WORLD?

Lives in Africa south of the Sahara, mostly along the Nile River. It was once spread through much of Africa.

ANIMAL FACTS

The name *hippopotamus* means *river horse*. Like horses, hippos live in herds of 5 to 30 animals. Hippos live in lakes, rivers, and streams near grasslands. They swim well and can also walk along the river bottom, staying submerged for up to six minutes. They are surprisingly fast on land, reaching a speed of about 20 miles (32 kilometers) per hour. Male hippos fiercely defend their *territory* (personal area), and can be dangerous to people. In fact, hippos kill more people than lions or crocodiles. Hippo numbers have fallen, mainly because of hunting by people.

Hippos have gaping jaws and long, sharp tusks.

SKIN
Glands (a type of organ) give off a reddish oil that protects the skin from the sun.

BODY
The body is large and barrel-shaped, with no hair except for a few bristles on the head and tail.

LEGS
The legs are short but powerful, allowing the hippopotamus to run quickly on land and swim well.

NOSTRILS
The nostrils are large and guarded by flaps that close when the hippopotamus is underwater.

HOW BIG IS IT?

HITCHING A RIDE
A young hippopotamus may rest on its mother's shoulders, especially in deeper waters, where the youngster cannot stand.

Duckbilled Platypus

VITAL STATISTICS

WEIGHT	About 5 lb (2.3 kg); males are larger
LENGTH	16–22 in (41–56 cm)
SEXUAL MATURITY	2 years
INCUBATION PERIOD	Eggs develop in the body for 28 days and are then incubated for 10 days
NUMBER OF OFFSPRING	1–3, emerging from their nesting burrow at about 4 months old
DIET	Eats insects, worms, and crayfish
LIFESPAN	Up to 11 years; 17 in captivity

The duckbilled platypus may be the most unusual mammal on Earth. It is one of the few mammals that lay eggs instead of bearing live young. The male also has *venomous* (poisonous) spurs on its hind legs.

WHERE IN THE WORLD?

Found only in eastern Australia, from eastern Queensland south to Victoria; also present on Tasmania.

ANIMAL FACTS

The platypus is a *monotreme,* a mammal that lays eggs. Except for platypuses and echidnas, all other monotremes died out millions of years ago. The platypus lives along streams with muddy bottoms. The bill has special sense organs that detect the electric signals given off by living things hidden in the mud. The platypus scoops up such prey with its bill. It lives in a *burrow* (underground shelter) dug into the bank of the stream. The burrow may be as long as 85 feet (26 meters).

The front claws are webbed for better swimming.

BILL
The rubbery bill is used to dig for food; the bill also has sense organs that help to find prey.

DENSE FUR
This traps air next to the body, keeping the platypus warm.

TAIL
Broad and flat, the tail helps the platypus steer itself underwater.

BREEDING BIOLOGY

Eggs measure about ½ inch (1.3 centimeters) across and have a leathery shell. The female *incubates* the eggs (keeps them warm) by curling around them. The young are blind and hairless when they hatch.

HOW BIG IS IT?

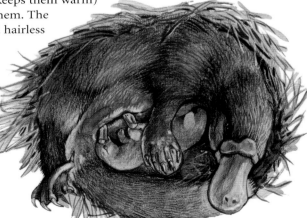

North American Mink

SPECIES • *Mustela vison*

VITAL STATISTICS

WEIGHT	1.5–3 lb (0.7–1.2 kg); males are heavier
LENGTH	20–25 in (50–64 cm)
SEXUAL MATURITY	Females 12 months; males 18 months
LENGTH OF PREGNANCY	30 days; development may not start for a month after fertilization
NUMBER OF OFFSPRING	2–8, average 4; weaning occurs at 6 weeks
DIET	Hunts small mammals, crayfish, ducks, fish, frogs, and reptiles
LIFESPAN	2–3 years; up to 8 years in captivity

The North American mink hunts both on land and in the water. It does not see well in the water, so the mink usually spots prey from the shore and then dives in to catch it.

WHERE IN THE WORLD?

Found across most of North America, apart from southwestern areas. Introduced to Europe and South America for ranching.

ANIMAL FACTS

The American mink is usually found in wooded areas near rivers, lakes, and marshes. On land, the mink hunts under logs, between rocks, and in rodent *burrows* (underground shelters). The mink is rarely attacked by other animals. People have long trapped minks for their fur. Today, minks are also ranched for their fur. American minks that escaped from European mink ranches and established wild populations have driven the European mink almost to extinction.

The European mink (bottom) has more white on the snout than the American mink (top).

FUR
The water-repellent fur is dense and glossy, varying from light to dark brown.

FACIAL COLORATION
The absence of white fur on the upper lips indicates that this is a North American rather than a European mink, which is also slightly smaller.

SITTING PRETTY
American minks can support themselves on their hindquarters.

PAWS
Partially webbed paws help the mink to swim well.

EYES AND EARS
The rounded eyes are small and dark; the ears are set well back on the head.

HOW BIG IS IT?

HUNTING SKILLS
Minks are fast, graceful hunters both on land and in the water. They catch crayfish, ducks, frogs, and fish from the water.

Otter

VITAL STATISTICS

WEIGHT	15–22 lb (7–10 kg); males are heavier
LENGTH	1.9–2.3 ft (57–70 cm); up to 12 in (30 cm) tall
SEXUAL MATURITY	2 years
LENGTH OF PREGNANCY	63 days; development does not begin right after fertilization
NUMBER OF OFFSPRING	2–3; *weaning* (to stop feeding on mother's milk) occurs at around 70 days
DIET	Eats mainly fish; also feeds on clams, crayfish, small mammals and amphibians, birds, insects, and worms
LIFESPAN	5–10 years in the wild; up to 20 in captivity

ANIMAL FACTS

The European otter is usually solitary and active at night. It hunts in fresh water and nests on nearby land. Otters can stay underwater for up to four minutes, but they usually hunt from the shore. The number of these animals has fallen, mainly because of damage to rivers, including water pollution and the construction of dams and canals. Otters are also killed by traps and fishing nets.

The otter's paw is webbed for better swimming.

Otters are playful animals that are often seen sliding down mudbanks or snowdrifts on their bellies. This behavior is thought to help young otters learn hunting techniques.

WHERE IN THE WORLD?

Lives across Europe north into Scandinavia, across Asia into China and Korea. Also found in northwestern North Africa.

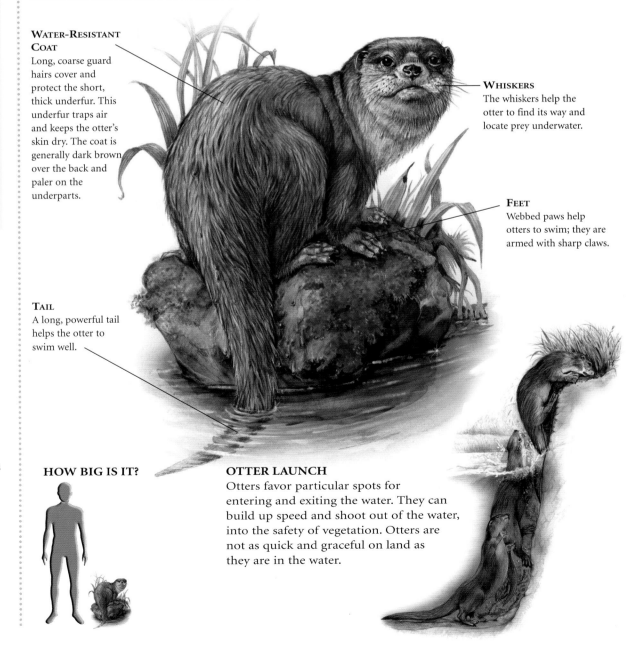

WATER-RESISTANT COAT
Long, coarse guard hairs cover and protect the short, thick underfur. This underfur traps air and keeps the otter's skin dry. The coat is generally dark brown over the back and paler on the underparts.

WHISKERS
The whiskers help the otter to find its way and locate prey underwater.

FEET
Webbed paws help otters to swim; they are armed with sharp claws.

TAIL
A long, powerful tail helps the otter to swim well.

HOW BIG IS IT?

OTTER LAUNCH
Otters favor particular spots for entering and exiting the water. They can build up speed and shoot out of the water, into the safety of vegetation. Otters are not as quick and graceful on land as they are in the water.

Giant Otter

SPECIES • *Pteronura brasiliensis*

The giant otter can reach 8 feet (2.4 meters) long and weigh up to 100 pounds (45 kilograms). This magnificent beast has become endangered, mainly because of *poaching* (illegal hunting) for its fur.

VITAL STATISTICS

WEIGHT	50–70 lb (22–32 kg); males are heavier
LENGTH	5–6 ft (1.5–1.8 m)
SEXUAL MATURITY	2 years
LENGTH OF PREGNANCY	65–70 days
NUMBER OF OFFSPRING	1–5, but averages 2; *weaning* (to stop feeding on mother's milk) occurs at 36 weeks
DIET	Feeds mainly on fish
LIFESPAN	5–8 years in the wild; up to 17 in captivity

WHERE IN THE WORLD?

Found in northern and central parts of South America.

ANIMAL FACTS

Giant otters live in extended family groups, with parents and offspring. The group clears an area along the river and digs a large *burrow* (underground shelter), often under a log. They also mark this *territory* (personal area) with scent. The group drives away any other giant otters that enter this territory. Giant otters are active during the day and hunt mainly by sight. The group maintains contact with a variety of calls. At times, the group works together to fish. Giant otters are *endangered* (in danger of dying out), mainly because of *poaching* (illegal hunting). People also have polluted many of the rivers where otters live.

Giant otters call to each other to maintain contact.

HEIGHT
The largest giant otters can stand as tall as a person's shoulders, though most are smaller.

MUZZLE
The muzzle is short and compact, giving the head a round appearance.

KEEPING IN TOUCH
All otter *species* (types) have a warning growl. Otters also use various kinds of chirps, chuckles, screams, and squeals to communicate.

FUR
The fur is normally chocolate-brown, but it can vary from fawn to red. It appears much darker when wet.

FEET
The large feet have webbing between the toes for better swimming.

HOW BIG IS IT?

HUNTING
The giant otter swims at the surface in clear waters, relying on its sharp vision to find fish swimming in the shallows. Then, the giant otter dives and snatches its prey.

Capybara

VITAL STATISTICS

WEIGHT	75–145 lb (35–66 kg)
LENGTH	Up to 4 ft (1.2 m)
SEXUAL MATURITY	Around 22 months for both sexes
LENGTH OF PREGNANCY	130–150 days
NUMBER OF OFFSPRING	Typically 4, but can be 2–8; *weaning* (to stop feeding on mother's milk) occurs after about 16 weeks
DIET	Eats grass, herbs, and *aquatic* (water) plants
LIFESPAN	5–7 years; up to 15 in captivity

The capybara is the largest rodent in the world. It grows up to 4 feet (1.2 meters) long and may weigh more than 100 pounds (45 kilograms). Capybaras are also called "water pigs" or "water hogs."

WHERE IN THE WORLD?

Lives in South America, east of the Andes.

ANIMAL FACTS

Capybaras are found in marshes or along rivers and streams. They live in groups of 10 to 30 adults. The group is led by the strongest male, who fights other males for leadership. Capybaras are most active at night. They are strong swimmers that often plunge into the water during the hottest part of the day. Capybaras also escape into water at any sign of trouble, though anacondas and *crocodilians* (a type of reptile) may lurk there. The greatest threat to the capybara is human hunting.

The capybara's teeth continue to grow throughout its life, so they do not wear away.

HAIR
This is coarse and thin, so adults roll in mud to protect against sunburn. The coat is reddish-brown or gray on its upper parts and yellowish-brown on its underparts.

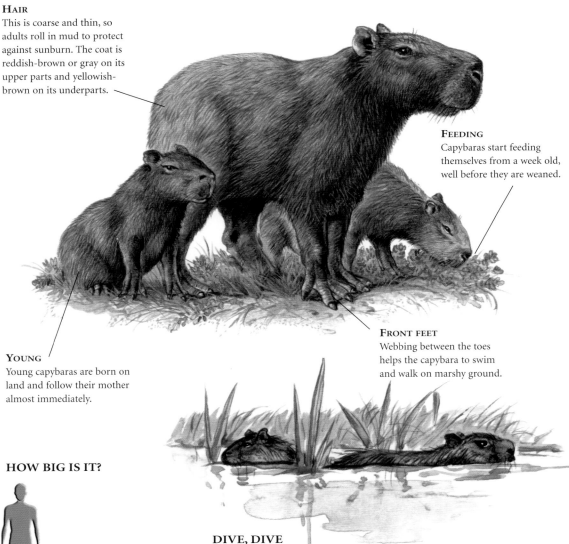

FEEDING
Capybaras start feeding themselves from a week old, well before they are weaned.

FRONT FEET
Webbing between the toes helps the capybara to swim and walk on marshy ground.

YOUNG
Young capybaras are born on land and follow their mother almost immediately.

HOW BIG IS IT?

DIVE, DIVE
Capybaras dive into the water at any sign of trouble. They can hide with just their eyes and nostrils above the surface. They can remain completely submerged for up to five minutes in order to escape *predators* (hunting animals).

North American Beaver

SPECIES • *Castor canadensis*

VITAL STATISTICS

WEIGHT	35–70 lb (16–32 kg)
LENGTH	3-4 ft (90–120 cm) including tail
SEXUAL MATURITY	1.5–2 years
LENGTH OF PREGNANCY	About 106 days
NUMBER OF OFFSPRING	2–3, but can be up to 8 kits per litter, born in late spring
DIET	Feeds on wood and water plants
LIFESPAN	10–15 years

Beavers use their strong jaws and *incisors* (cutting teeth) to cut down trees to build dams. The dams create small ponds that support many other living things, including amphibians, birds, fish, and insects.

WHERE IN THE WORLD?

Found throughout most of North America, from Alaska and Canada south to Florida and Mexico.

ANIMAL FACTS

By building dams, beavers create the ponds they need to thrive. The dam is made of tree branches and rocks plastered together with mud. Beavers typically appear busy working on their dams or lodges. For this reason, people often call a hard-working person an "eager beaver" or say that the person is as "busy as a beaver." Beaver ponds provide a home for many other living things. After the dam breaks and the pond drains, the rich soil left behind supports beautiful meadows. People have long trapped beavers for their valuable fur. Trapping had wiped out beavers from many areas by 1900. Since then, beavers have recovered in most areas.

COAT
Dense and waterproof, the coat is typically reddish-brown, but its color varies from yellowish to black.

FACE
The rounded ears and small nostrils can close tightly to keep out water.

WOODY DIET
Microbes (germs) in the beaver's gut help it digest bark, twigs, leaves, and roots of trees and shrubs.

TAIL
The large, flat tail acts like a paddle and a rudder for the beaver. Beavers are more graceful in the water than they are on land.

THE LODGE

Beavers build a sturdy home called a lodge. The lodge can be entered only from beneath the water, offering protection from *predators* (hunting animals).

Beaver parents care for their young for about two years.

HOW BIG IS IT?

Muskrat

VITAL STATISTICS

WEIGHT	1.5–4 lb (0.7–1.8 kg)
LENGTH	16–24 in (40–60 cm) overall; tail is almost as long as the body
SEXUAL MATURITY	By 4 months
LENGTH OF PREGNANCY	25–30 days; 1–5 litters annually
NUMBER OF OFFSPRING	4–7, but can be up to 11; weaning occurs at 3–4 weeks
DIET	Mainly eats cattails and water plants; some small animals
LIFESPAN	3–4 years

These rodents fight a great deal among themselves. Many of them travel about—even as far as 20 miles (32 kilometers)—to find new homes.

WHERE IN THE WORLD?

Found across much of North America, from Alaska south to Mexico and the Gulf Coast.

ANIMAL FACTS

Muskrats live in family groups made up of a breeding pair and their offspring. The group defends a *territory* (personal area), which is marked by oily *musk* (scent). Muskrats are eaten by a variety of animals, including alligators, owls, snakes, and raccoons. Muskrats flee into the water when threatened and can stay under for more than 10 minutes. Some people eat the flesh of muskrats, which may be called "marsh rabbit." Muskrats have been introduced to Asia, Europe, and South America. Although the muskrat is a rodent, it is not a true rat.

In cross-section, the height of the tail is greater than its width, forming a paddle for swimming.

FUR
Thick and double-layered, the brown fur repels water.

EARS
The small ears seal shut when the muskrat is submerged.

FRONT PAWS
Equipped with sharp claws, these allow the muskrat to hold the plants it feeds on. The animals sometimes eat clams, crayfish, and snails.

TAIL
The tail is covered with scales rather than hair.

LODGES
Muskrat homes are made of mud and vegetation. In winter, the underwater entrances may be closed to keep the inside warm.

HOW BIG IS IT?

European Water Vole

VITAL STATISTICS

WEIGHT	2.5–9 oz (70–250 g)
LENGTH	5–9 in (12–22 cm) overall; tail is slightly shorter than the body
SEXUAL MATURITY	After the first winter
LENGTH OF PREGNANCY	21 days; 2–5 litters annually
NUMBER OF OFFSPRING	Up to 8; weaning occurs after about 56 days
DIET	Eats mainly grass and herbs
LIFESPAN	Up to 5 years

ANIMAL FACTS

The European water vole usually lives in small family groups, with two parents and their offspring. This group defends a *territory* (personal area), marking it with a scent made by *glands* (a type of organ). The voles dig *burrows* (underground shelters) in the banks of rivers, streams, or ponds. In areas where food is abundant, water voles can have a population boom. They may become so numerous that they damage fields and forests by eating too many plants. In most cases, water vole numbers are controlled by *predators* (hunting animals). Many predators, including minks, otters, and herons, hunt these rodents. Most water voles do not survive for even a year.

The European water vole is a rodent that lives in the banks of rivers, streams, and ponds. It is an excellent swimmer that uses the water to escape from *predators* (hunting animals).

WHERE IN THE WORLD?

Found across much of Europe and northern Asia.

FUR
The overall color is dark brown, but the underside is lighter.

NOSE
This is more rounded and shorter in appearance than that of a rat.

FRONT PAWS
These can be used like hands to hold food.

EARS
The ears are low and blend in with the head.

HUNTED
Storks and other hunting animals feed on these rodents and prevent them from becoming too numerous.

HOW BIG IS IT?

GNAWING AWAY
Water voles often dig beneath the surface to feed on roots, which can kill young trees and shrubs. In this way, water voles can have a significant impact on the landscape.

Nutria

The nutria, which is also called the "coypu," is a South American rodent that lives along the banks of lakes, marshes, and rivers. The nutria has now spread to many other parts of the world.

VITAL STATISTICS

WEIGHT	11–22 lb (5–10 kg); males slightly larger
LENGTH	About 40 in (100 cm) including tail
SEXUAL MATURITY	Females 3–9 months; males 4–9 months
LENGTH OF PREGNANCY	About 130 days; 2 litters a year
NUMBER OF OFFSPRING	Average 4–5, but ranges from 1–13; weaning occurs at 56–63 days
DIET	Eats mainly water plants
LIFESPAN	Up to 6 years

WHERE IN THE WORLD?

Native to southern South America, the nutria has been introduced to Asia, Europe, and North America.

ANIMAL FACTS

Nutrias have been prized for their fur, which is made into coats and gloves. Nutrias have spread to new areas because people have tried to raise the animals on farms. Inevitably, the nutrias escaped. After they have become established in an area, nutrias are difficult to remove. Unfortunately, they can damage native wildlife by eating too many *aquatic* (water) plants. They also feed on such crops as rice and sugar cane. Finally, they may dig *burrows* (underground shelters) into earthen dams, weakening the dams and even causing flooding.

Nutria are born ready for action. They *nurse* (drink milk from their mother) for only about two months.

PROFILE
The nutria has a hunched body shape because the hind legs are longer than the front legs.

TAIL
The tail has a relatively thick covering of hair. The tail makes up nearly half the total length of the body.

HIND FEET
Four webbed toes are equipped with sharp claws, alongside a single smaller toe.

EYES
These are positioned relatively high on the head, giving good visibility when the nutria is partly submerged.

MUZZLE
The nutria has a whitish-tipped muzzle.

HOW BIG IS IT?

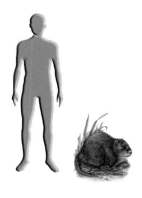

NUTRIA BURROWS

In some areas, nutria burrows have weakened earthen dams. Nutrias can even cause such dams to fail, flooding nearby land.

Eurasian Water Shrew

SPECIES · *Neomys fodiens*

The Eurasian water shrew looks like a mouse with a sharp nose. It is one of the few mammals able to produce *venom* (poison), which it uses to stun the small *aquatic* (water) animals it preys on.

VITAL STATISTICS

WEIGHT	About 0.5 oz (15 g)
LENGTH	7 in (17.5 cm) overall; the tail is about three-quarters of the length
SEXUAL MATURITY	By 3.5 months
LENGTH OF PREGNANCY	20 days; 2–3 litters a year, born in a nest of grass
NUMBER OF OFFSPRING	Average 5–6, range 3–12; weaning occurs at 42 days
DIET	Eats mainly snails, insects, and mollusks; some fish and frogs
LIFESPAN	Up to 18 months

WHERE IN THE WORLD?

Found thoughout much of Europe and northern Asia, reaching the Pacific coast of Asia.

ANIMAL FACTS

The teeth of the Eurasian water shrew have red tips. This coloration is caused by iron, which helps to strengthen the teeth. Eurasian water shrews are often solitary and occupy *territories* (personal areas). They live in *burrows* (underground shelters). They are active both during the day and at night. They search for prey and must eat about half their body weight every day. These shrews also serve as food for many other animals. They are eaten by snakes, owls, and weasels, among other *predators* (hunting animals).

COLORATION
The upperparts have short, dark fur. The underside is white.

FUR
The fur traps air, which helps the shrew to float but makes diving more difficult.

EYES AND EARS
The eyes are small, as are the ears, which are largely hidden by fur.

HEAD
The snout is long, with a pink tip on the nose.

HOW BIG IS IT?

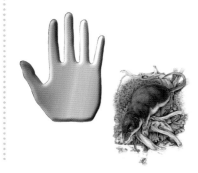

SWIMMING
Bristles on the underside of the tail and on the paws act to push the water backward, helping the shrew to swim well.

Mallard

VITAL STATISTICS

WEIGHT	2.25–3.25 lb (1–1.5 kg)
LENGTH	20–30 in (51–71 cm)
SEXUAL MATURITY	Usually at 2 years old
HATCHING PERIOD	28 days
NUMBER OF EGGS	7–16, buff to grayish-green in color
DIET	Feeds on insects, snails, and small water animals; also eats seeds and plants
LIFESPAN	Averages 7–10 years

ANIMAL FACTS

Mallards thrive in shallow wetlands. Although mallards fly well, they spend most of their time floating on the water. Their webbed feet enable them to swim well. The female has a dull brown color that serves as *camouflage* (disguise). After the breeding season, the male loses its bright feathers and looks much like the female. The familiar "quack" of ducks is made by the female mallard. She quacks to call her ducklings. The birds *migrate* (travel) with the changing seasons, heading south in the fall. Mallards are abundant and widespread. Although hunters take millions of mallards each year, the ducks are not *threatened* (in danger of dying out). Mallards have been introduced to Australia and New Zealand.

The mallard is the most widely recognized duck. Only the breeding male has metallic green feathers on the head. He also has a white neck ring and a chestnut breast.

WHERE IN THE WORLD?

Widely spread in northern areas, including Asia, Europe, and North America.

WING COLORATION
This brightly colored bar across the wings is most evident in flight.

COLORATION
Breeding males have metallic green feathers on the head.

FEET
Webbing between the toes helps the ducks swim more easily. There are claws at the end of the toes.

TAIL
Males have curled tail feathers.

HOW BIG IS IT?

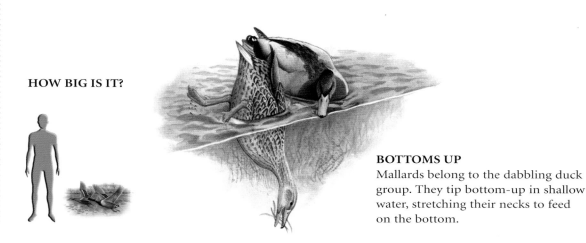

BOTTOMS UP
Mallards belong to the dabbling duck group. They tip bottom-up in shallow water, stretching their necks to feed on the bottom.

Greater Flamingo

SPECIES • *Phoenicopterus roseus*

VITAL STATISTICS

WEIGHT	4–9 lb (2–4 kg)
HEIGHT	3–5 ft (91–150 cm); wingspan 60 in (152 cm)
SEXUAL MATURITY	3–5 years
NUMBER OF EGGS	1–2; may breed twice annually
INCUBATION PERIOD	27–30 days;
DIET	Filters for tiny water animals and algae
LIFESPAN	Up to 20 years

Flamingos are born gray and only turn pinkish-red as they mature. Their coloration comes from the tiny, shrimplike animals they eat.

WHERE IN THE WORLD?

Found along the southeast Atlantic coast of North America, down through the Caribbean and into northern South America.

ANIMAL FACTS

Flamingos live in large colonies that can number many thousands of individuals. They tend to occupy large mudflats near a food supply. They almost always live in coastal areas, and they favor shallow water where they can wade and feed. The special filtering plates in their bills enable them to feed on the smallest water animals. Flamingos all breed at the same time, shaping the mud into walled nests. The chicks hatch with gray feathers. They are protected by the adult birds as they grow. The pink coloration of adults comes from a *pigment* (coloring) found in the shrimp-like animals they eat.

NECK
The long and flexible neck enables the bird to stand and still reach the water to feed.

NOSTRILS
These are long slits. Flamingos do not rely on their sense of smell.

BILL
Thick with a down-curving tip, the bill is used to filter the water for food.

LEGS
The legs are long and straight, helping these birds to move easily through shallow water.

NESTING
The female constructs a dome-shaped nest of mud, about 10 inches (25 centimeters) high. The nest's elevation protects it from being flooded.

The bill has filtering plates called *lamellae*, which trap tiny water animals.

HOW BIG IS IT?

PAIRING
A strong bond exists in flamingo pairs. Mates engage in elaborate courtship dances during the breeding season.

Ruff

VITAL STATISTICS

WEIGHT	5–6 oz (150–170 g)
LENGTH	Males 11–13 in (28–32 cm); females are somewhat smaller
SEXUAL MATURITY	By 3 years
NUMBER OF EGGS	3–4, light brown with darker blotches
INCUBATION PERIOD	28–30 days; young fledge at around 26 days
DIET	Eats mainly insects and other tiny animals; also some plants
LIFESPAN	Up to 14 years

ANIMAL FACTS

The coloring of the breeding male varies to an unusual degree among ruffs. Some males, called resident males, have chestnut or black ruffs. They make courtship displays on breeding grounds called *leks*. Other males have white ruffs and are known as satellite males. They do not have a *territory* (personal area) on the breeding grounds. Still other males have feathers like those of females, helping them to sneak in among the hens unchallenged by other males. All ruffs feed in wetlands and shallow waters, wading to take insects and other small animals.

The feathers are sleek in flight, to minimize air resistance.

The ruff is a wading bird that gathers in huge flocks on its winter grounds in Africa. These flocks may include up to 1 million birds. In the summer, they have a complex mating ritual.

WHERE IN THE WORLD?

Spends the summer in the far north of Europe and Asia and overwinters in southern Europe and Africa.

DISPLAY
The breeding male has a neck ruff of longer feathers and elaborate head tufts.

BILL
The bill is straight and tapers along its length.

WHITE AREAS
These white markings across the flight feathers show up as oval streaks in flight.

LEGS
The yellow legs are long, like those of most wading birds.

BREEDING FEATHERS
Breeding males sport an unusual variety of feathers.

HOW BIG IS IT?

THE RUFF'S NAME

The longer feathers around the male's neck resemble a ruff, the large and elaborate collar once worn by aristocrats in Europe.

Hoatzin

The hoatzin is an unusual-looking bird of South America that feeds mainly on vegetation in wetlands and along streams. The young have small claws on their wings which help them to climb trees.

VITAL STATISTICS

WEIGHT	About 30 oz (793 g)
LENGTH	25 in (65 cm) overall
SEXUAL MATURITY	Around 2 years
NUMBER OF EGGS	2–3, cream with brown, blue, or pinkish spotting
INCUBATION PERIOD	28 days; young fledge around 10–14 days, before they are fully developed
DIET	Feeds mainly on marsh and wetland plants
LIFESPAN	20 years in the wild; up to 30 in captivity

ANIMAL FACTS

Hoatzins are unusual among birds in that they eat leaves as well as fruit and flowers. Their digestive system is also unique among birds—they have a *crop*, like that found in cattle and other grazing animals. The crop contains *microbes* (germs) that help to break down plant matter. The process creates an unpleasant odor, so these birds are also called "stinkbirds." Hoatzin chicks have claws on their wings that help them to climb trees before they are able to fly. The earliest birds, which lived during the time of the dinosaurs, also had claws on their wings.

A cross-section of the crop, with food inside.

WHERE IN THE WORLD?

Lives in northern South America, in the Amazon rain forest.

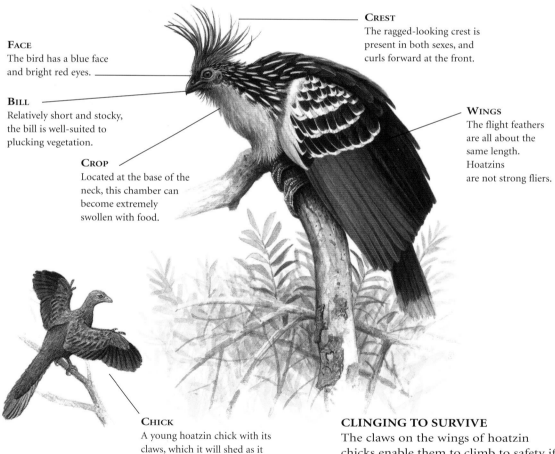

FACE
The bird has a blue face and bright red eyes.

BILL
Relatively short and stocky, the bill is well-suited to plucking vegetation.

CROP
Located at the base of the neck, this chamber can become extremely swollen with food.

CREST
The ragged-looking crest is present in both sexes, and curls forward at the front.

WINGS
The flight feathers are all about the same length. Hoatzins are not strong fliers.

CHICK
A young hoatzin chick with its claws, which it will shed as it matures.

HOW BIG IS IT?

CLINGING TO SURVIVE
The claws on the wings of hoatzin chicks enable them to climb to safety if they fall into the water.

Sunbittern

VITAL STATISTICS

WEIGHT	About 7.5 oz (210 g)
LENGTH	18–21 in (46–53 cm)
SEXUAL MATURITY	2 years
NUMBER OF EGGS	2, buff with dark spotting
INCUBATION PERIOD	About 27 days; fledging occurs at 17–24 days;
DIET	Hunts insects and other small animals
LIFESPAN	10 years; up to 17 years in captivity

The sunbittern gets its name from the sun-like markings on its wings. These patterns are actually *eyespots* (eye-like markings), which the bird uses in both courtship and displays to threaten other birds.

WHERE IN THE WORLD?

Found in northern South America, in the Amazon rain forest and in parts of Central America.

ANIMAL FACTS

The sunbittern lives near streams and marshy areas, but it wades rather than swims, plucking prey from the water with its spear-like bill. At the start of the breeding season, the male displays the vibrant colors of his wings and tail. The domed nest, made from grass and mud, may be constructed either on the ground or in the branch of a tree or shrub. *Predators* (hunting animals) that threaten the sunbittern may be startled by flashes of its wings. The large eyespots on the wings may give the impression of a much larger animal.

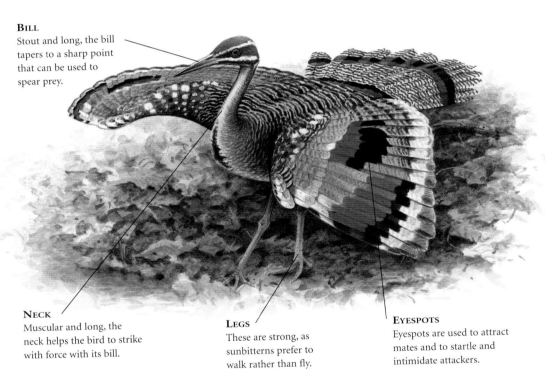

BILL
Stout and long, the bill tapers to a sharp point that can be used to spear prey.

NECK
Muscular and long, the neck helps the bird to strike with force with its bill.

LEGS
These are strong, as sunbitterns prefer to walk rather than fly.

EYESPOTS
Eyespots are used to attract mates and to startle and intimidate attackers.

The wings have striking colors and eyespots.

HOW BIG IS IT?

HUNTING STRATEGY

The sunbittern is a watchful hunter, waiting for signs of movement in the water. When it spots prey, the bird walks over slowly and then strikes without warning. The spear-like bill is a lethal weapon.

Kingfisher

SPECIES • *Alcedo atthis*

VITAL STATISTICS

WEIGHT	1–1.5 oz (26–39 g)
LENGTH	6.5–7 in (16–18 cm)
SEXUAL MATURITY	Likely to breed in the year after hatching
NUMBER OF EGGS	6–7, white in color
INCUBATION PERIOD	19–21 days; young fledge by 27 days, and the adult pair breeds up to 3 times annually
DIET	Eats mainly fish and shrimplike animals
LIFESPAN	7–15 years

ANIMAL FACTS

The kingfisher is most common along slow-flowing stretches of streams and lakes. The bird typically perches on an overhanging branch to watch the water below. Its eyes are especially *adapted* (suited) to spotting prey in the water—they can filter out the glare of the sun on the surface. The bird is also an expert at gauging the position of a fish, despite the distortion of the water. Although kingfishers remain common, water pollution threatens them in some areas.

A young kingfisher lacks the metallic blue feathers found in the adult.

The kingfisher is a colorful bird that perches near streams and lakes, watching for fish. When it spots prey, the bird plunges into the water, diving to catch its food.

WHERE IN THE WORLD?

Found in much of Europe and Asia, into northern Africa and Indonesia.

NOSTRILS
These slits are at the base of the bill.

BILL
This is completely black in males, while females have a reddish-orange base to the bill.

EYES
The eyes are protected by a thin layer of tissue that covers them when the bird dives underwater.

BACK
The back is metallic blue, a color that extends to the head.

BREEDING HABITS

The kingfisher digs a tunnel in the river bank. The bird creates a nesting chamber where the eggs can hatch and the chicks can grow.

HOW BIG IS IT?

HUNTING TECHNIQUE

A kingfisher waits on a perch, watching for fish.

The bird plunges down, folding its wings back as it dives.

The kingfisher uses its spear-like bill to catch fish.

It breaks the surface and returns to its perch.

The kingfisher beats the fish against the branch to stun it, and then the bird swallows the fish headfirst.

Glossary

adaptation a characteristic of a living thing that makes it better able to survive and reproduce in its environment

amphibian one of a group of cold-blooded animals with a backbone and moist, smooth skin; many amphibians are born in the water and later live on land

anal fin a fin located at the back of the fish

anglers people who fish

aquatic plants plants that grow or live in water

barbells whisker-like growths on some animals that serve as sense organs

burrows underground shelters that an animal uses as a home or hiding place

camouflage protective coloration that makes an animal difficult for a predator to see

constrictor type of snake that kills its prey by squeezing it with its coils

crocodilian a type of reptile that belongs to the group that includes crocodiles, alligators, and gavials

dorsal fin a fin located on or near the back

echolocation a method of finding the direction and distance of objects through echoes

eyespots eye-like markings on birds, butterflies, fish, and reptiles that are used in courtship or to frighten predators

elytra the pair of thickened front wings of beetles and other insects that form a protective covering for the back wings

fish fry the young of fish

game wild animals, birds, or fish hunted or caught for sport or for food

gills part of the body of a fish, tadpole, crab, or other animal that lives in water by which the animal breathes in water

glands organs that make a particular substance that the body needs

habitat the kind of place in which an animal lives

hibernate to live in a sleep-like state during the winter

incubate to keep fertilized eggs and young animals under proper conditions for growth and development

incisors teeth that have a sharp edge for cutting

lamellae thin plates or layers of flesh and bone that serve different purposes in such animals as water birds and crabs

larva the immature form of certain animals, which differs from the adult form in many ways

metamorphosis a series of stages in the development of some animals from their immature form to adulthood

microbes very small living things; germs

migration the movement of animals from place to place to avoid unfavorable changes in weather or food supply, or to take advantage of better living conditions

molting the process of shedding feathers, skin, hair, shell, antlers, or other growths before a new growth

monotreme a type of mammal that gives birth by laying eggs; the echidna and the platypus are the only monotremes living today

musk a substance with a strong and lasting odor found in a special gland in some animals, including musk deer, mink, muskrats, and peccaries

nuptial pads toe swellings that toads, frogs, and salamanders develop during breeding season

nurse to drink milk from a mother

nymph insect stage of development between egg and adult

parotid glands glands located near the ear that, in toads and some frogs and salamanders, produce poisons that make the skin taste bad to predators

pigment the natural substance occurring in and coloring the tissues of an animal or plant

poaching hunting in an area or at a time when it is illegal to do so

predators animals that prey upon other animals

pupa inactive stage in the development of some animals, particularly insects

reptiles animals with dry, scaly skin that breathe through lungs

scutes hard, shield-like structures that make up the outer layer of skin of some turtles, armadillos, and crocodiles

spawn to lay eggs

species a kind of living thing; members of a species share many characteristics and are able to interbreed

spurs remnants of legs found near the tails of some snakes

territory the area in which an animal lives and which it defends

threatened a term used by conservationists to indicate that a species is in danger of dying out; threatened species are further classified as "least concern," "near threatened," "vulnerable," "endangered," and "critically endangered"

top predator an animal that feeds on a variety of other animals but which other animals do not prey on

tympanum a disk of skin behind the eyes of most frogs that serves as an eardrum

venom a poisonous substance produced by many kinds of animals to injure, kill, or digest prey

ventral fin a fin located on the abdomen

vocal sac loose folds of skin on each side of the mouth in many male frogs that allows them to amplify their call

wean to accustom a young animal to food other than its mother's milk

Resources

Books

Everglades Forever: Restoring America's Great Wetland
by Trish Marx and Cindy Karp (Lee & Low Books, 2004)
Follow along with a group of students as they travel to the Everglades, learning about the threats this wetland faces and how people can help preserve it.

A Journey into a Wetland by Rebecca L. Johnson
and Phyllis V. Saroff (Carolrhoda Books, 2004)
This book examines the ways in which the many plant and animal residents of a swamp are connected.

Lakes and Rivers: A Freshwater Web of Life
by Philip Johansson (Enslow Publishers, 2008)
Learn about the food webs that exist in our lake and river biomes.

River Wild: An Activity Guide to North American Rivers
by Nancy F. Castaldo (Chicago Review Press, 2006)
Games and activities provide an interactive introduction to rivers in North America and the habitats that surround them.

Websites

BBC Nature: Rivers and Streams
http://www.bbc.co.uk/nature/habitats/River
Videos, articles, and images introduce readers to freshwater habitats around the world.

National Wildlife Foundation: What's a Wetland?
http://www.nwf.org/Kids/Ranger-Rick/People-and-Places/Whats-a-Wetland.aspx
Students can learn about the many different kinds of wetlands, and what can be done to protect them, at this educational website.

Rivers and Streams: Water Science for Schools
http://ga.water.usgs.gov/edu/earthrivers.html
Diagrams and links at this website from the United States Geological Survey teach about the formation and uses of rivers, streams, and other freshwater resources.

Acknowledgments

Cover photograph: Masterfile (Minden Pictures)

Illustrations: © Art-Tech

Photographs:

Corbis RF: 29

Dreamstime: 8 (T. Haynes), 12 (S. Dunn), 15 (S. Dunn), 17 (S. Siloto), 22 (B. MacQueen), 23 (H. Leyrer), 25 (M. Ushakov), 29 (S. Pettitt), 42 (N. Smit), 45 (Z. Camernik)

FLPA: 6 (G. Lacz), 9 (W. Meinderts), 10 (Silvestris), 11 (J. de Cuveland), 13 (D. Usher), 20 (C. Mattison), 21 (N. Cattlin), 26 (H. Koch), 27 (N. Wu), 30 (Foto Natura), 37 (M. B. Withers), 39 (P. Oakenfull)

Fotolia: 7 (M. Wear), 33 (M. Lopez)

iStock Photo: 43 (M. Bruce)

Photos.com: 14, 16, 18, 24, 31, 35, 36, 40

Stock.Xchng: 34 (Q. Kuiken)

Stockxpert: 41 (D. Thyberg)

U.S. Fish & Wildlife Services: 28, 38

Webshots: 44 (Jacob 79)

Index